FUN FIRST CONCE[PTS]

LET'S LEARN COUNTING

by Anna C. Peterson

MARCH 2021

TABLE OF CONTENTS

tadpole books

LET'S LEARN COUNTING!

I see one ball.

2

I see two balls.

3

I see three balls.

I see four balls.

I see five balls.

6

I see six balls.

I see seven balls.

8

I see eight balls.

9

I see nine balls.

I see ten balls.

LET'S REVIEW!

How many balls do you see below?

NUMBER CHART

1 2 3 4 5

6 7 8 9 10